accent on
Majors
for piano

by William Gillock

CONTENTS

ISBN 978-1-5400-2745-0

WILLIS MUSIC

EXCLUSIVELY DISTRIBUTED BY

HAL•LEONARD®

7777 W. BLUEMOUND RD. P.O. BOX 13819 MILWAUKEE, WI 53213

Visit Hal Leonard Online at
www.halleonard.com

Foreword

ACCENT ON MAJORS is a book with a purpose.

It is, first of all, a collection of literature for lower elementary level,[*] and secondly, a theory work book devoted to a better understanding of the keys and key signatures of the seven major scales which use as keynotes the seven white keys.

This presentation follows the recommended musicianship chart for the Elementary B level of the National Guild of Piano Teachers, and the pieces are of the required grade and length for auditions, as recommended in the suggested literature chart of this organization.

ACCENT ON MAJORS is meant to follow a basic reading course in which the player has learned simple extension and contraction, and some movement over the keyboard.

William Gillock

*These pieces would be considered later elementary to early intermediate level in today's leveling system (2018).

To MIRIAM HOPPER and TIMMY KOLP

PREPARATORY

What is the meaning of KEY?

A family of related tones (scale) and chords which come to a <u>restful</u> <u>sound</u> on a specific tonality is called the "KEY OF —" in music. The <u>restful</u> <u>sounding</u> tone or chord gives the key its name. This tone or chord can be identified by the feeling <u>you</u> have of having "arrived home" after a musical journey. (Test yourself by playing a scale you know: which tone of the scale sounds like the "home tone"?)

What is a SCALE?

An orderly sequence of tones within the compass of one octave is called a scale. The scales presented in this book are the familiar Major Scales which begin on the white keys of the piano. Each of these scales is made up of seven tones— one tone for each letter name of the musical alphabet. When you name the notes of the following scale, notice that you do not repeat a letter name (except for the first and last notes which are the same tone).

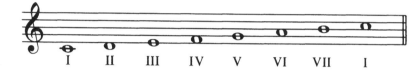

The tones of the scale are numbered with Roman Numerals to help us identify them. The "home tone" of each scale is always Roman Numeral I.

What are the CHORDS of a key?

Triads built on each tone of the scale are the chords of the key. Because the chords built on the I, IV and V tones of the scale are used in music more than the others, we shall learn these first.

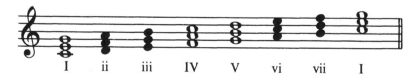

The I- Chord is called the Tonic Chord; the IV- Chord, Sub-Dominant; and the V- Chord, Dominant.

What is a CADENCE?

A sequence of chords which comes to rest on the Tonic Chord is called a cadence.
A cadence of I-IV-I sequence is called a Plagal Cadence; a cadence of I-V-I
sequence is called an Authentic Cadence. Here is an easy way to form these cadences:

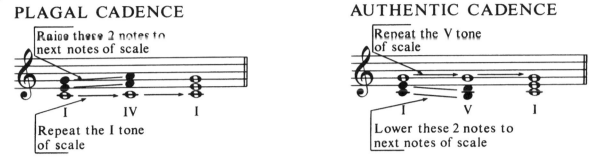

What is a KEY SIGNATURE?

The sharps or flats (or absence of these) at the beginning of each staff is called KEY
SIGNATURE. There may be as many as seven sharps or seven flats in a key signature,
but we shall learn only the first five at this time. Since you will be asked to write key
signatures on the following pages, PLAY on the keyboard and MEMORIZE the order
of the following sharps and flats:

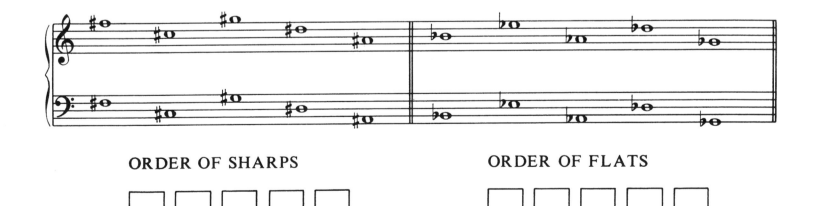

ORDER OF SHARPS

☐ ☐ ☐ ☐ ☐

ORDER OF FLATS

☐ ☐ ☐ ☐ ☐

KEY OF C MAJOR

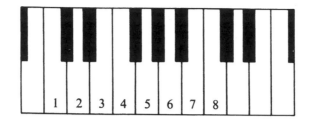

Write the names of the keys in the boxes

Here are the notes of the scale of C Major; the I, IV, V chords in root position, and two easy cadences. Practice the scale in the following rhythmic and harmonized presentation:

Practice the I, IV and V chords of the key of C Major in three positions, each, and the Plagal and Authentic cadences in root position. Can you tell which position of the IV chord is used in the Plagal cadence? Which position of the V chord is used in the Authentic cadence?

The following piece, DANCE THE WALTZ, is written in the key of C Major.

DANCE THE WALTZ

In waltz time (♩ = 176 - 184)

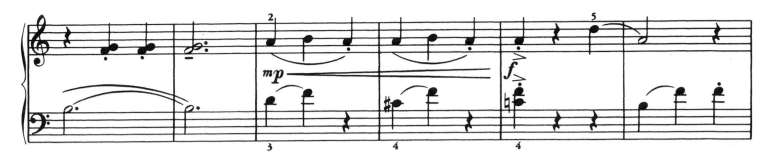

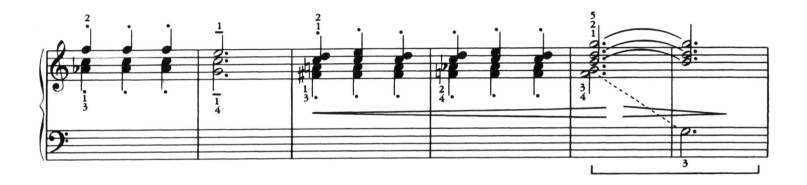

KEY OF G MAJOR

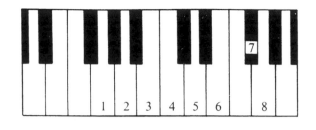

Write the names of the keys in the boxes

Here are the notes of the scale of G Major; the I, IV, V chords in root position and two easy cadences. Write the key signature at the beginning of each staff of the scale and the chord and cadence sequences. Circle the notes in the scale which will be played on black keys. Practice the scale in the following rhythmic and harmonized presentation:

Practice the I, IV and V chords of the key of G Major in <u>three</u> positions, each, and the Plagal and Authentic cadences in root position. Can you tell which position of the IV chord is used in the Plagal cadence? Which position of the V chord is used in the Authentic cadence?

CHORDS OF THE KEY
I ii iii IV V vi vii I

PLAGAL CADENCE
I IV I

AUTHENTIC CADENCE
I V I

The following piece, PIXIES, is written in the key of G Major. Before you play it, write the key signature at the beginning of each staff.

PIXIES

Playfully ($\boldsymbol{\mathcal{J}}$ = 104-112)

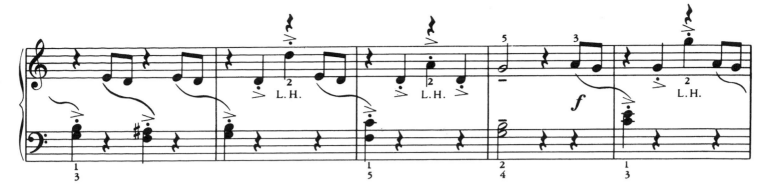

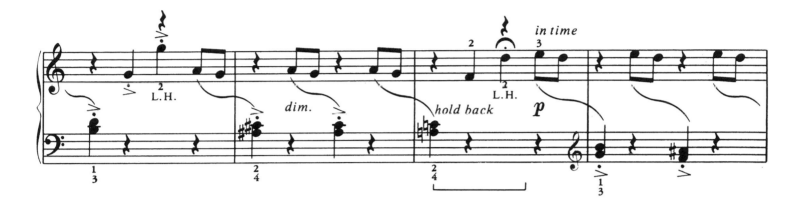

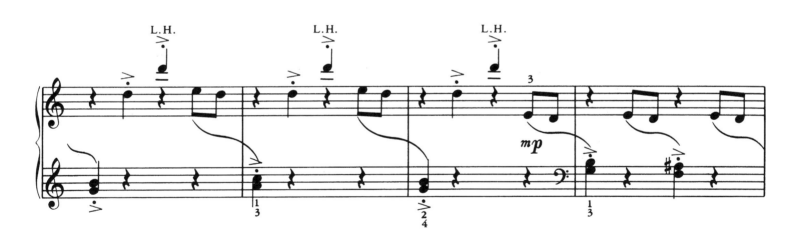

KEY OF D MAJOR

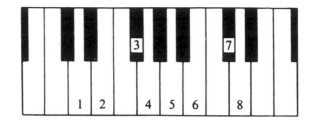

Write the names of the keys in the boxes

Here are the notes of the scale of D Major; the I, IV, V chords in root position, and two easy cadences. Write the key signature at the beginning of each staff of the scale and the chord and cadence sequences. Circle the notes in the scale which will be played on black keys. Practice the scale in the following rhythmic and harmonized presentation:

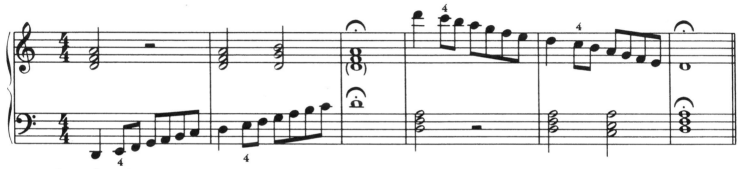

Practice the I, IV and V chords of the key of D Major in three positions, each, and the Plagal and Authentic cadences in root position. Can you tell which position of the IV chord is used in the Plagal cadence? Which position of the V chord is used in the Authentic cadence?

The following piece, CHILDREN SKATING, is written in the key of D Major. Before you play it, write the key signature at the beginning of each staff.

CHILDREN SKATING

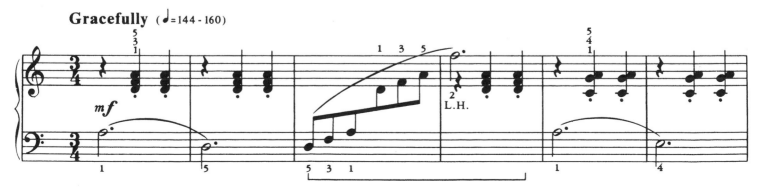

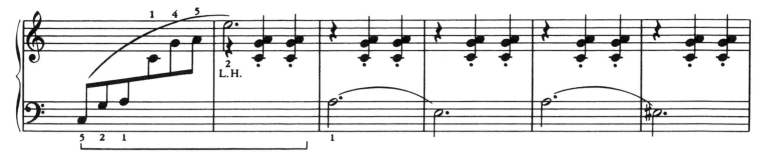

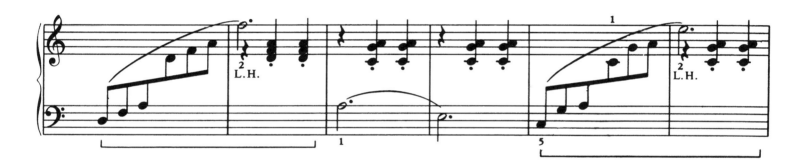

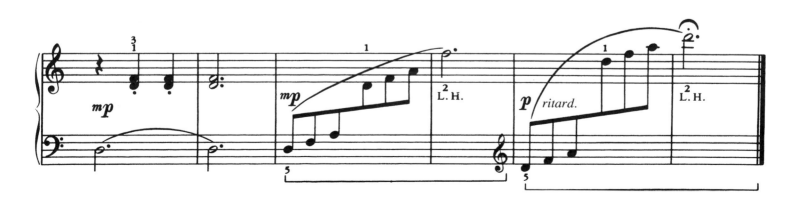

KEY OF A MAJOR

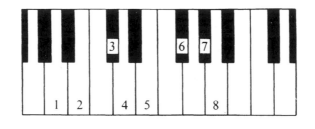

Write the names of the keys in the boxes

Here are the notes of the scale of A Major; the I, IV, V chords in root position, and two easy cadences. Write the key signature at the beginning of each staff of the scale and the chord and cadence sequences. Circle the notes in the scale which will be played on black keys. Practice the scale in the following rhythmic and harmonized presentation:

Practice the I, IV and V chords of the key of A Major in three positions, each, and the Plagal and Authentic cadences in root position. Can you tell which position of the IV chord is used in the Plagal cadence? Which position of the V chord is used in the Authentic cadence?

CHORDS OF THE KEY
I ii iii IV V vi vii I

PLAGAL CADENCE   AUTHENTIC CADENCE
I   IV   I   I   V   I

The following piece, CHRISTMAS TREE PARADE, is written in the key of A Major. Before you play it, write the key signature at the beginning of each staff.

CHRISTMAS TREE PARADE

In brisk march time   (♩ = 76-84)

KEY OF E MAJOR

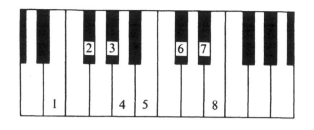

Write the names of the keys in the boxes

Here are the notes of the scale of E Major; the I, IV, V chords in root position, and two easy cadences. Write the key signature at the beginning of each staff of the scale and the chord and cadence sequences. Circle the notes in the scale which will be played on black keys. Practice the scale in the following rhythmic and harmonized presentation:

Practice the I, IV and V chords of the key of E Major in <u>three</u> positions, each, and the Plagal and Authentic cadences in root position. Can you tell which position of the IV chord is used in the Plagal cadence? Which position of the V chord is used in the Authentic cadence?

The following piece, IN SUNNY SPAIN, is written in the key of E Major. Before you play it, write the key signature at the beginning of each staff.

IN SUNNY SPAIN

Rhythmic, but not fast (♩=112-120)

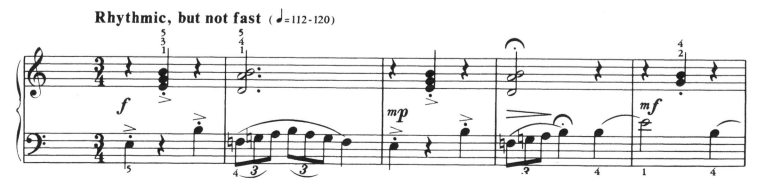

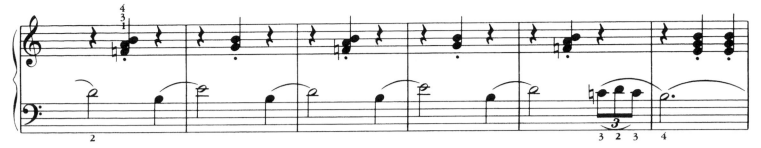

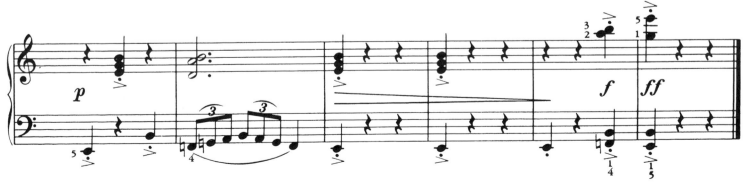

KEY OF B MAJOR

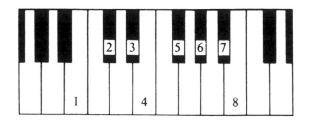

Write the names of the keys in the boxes

Here are the notes of the scale of **B Major**; the I, IV, V chords in root position, and two easy cadences. Write the key signature at the beginning of each staff of the scale and the chord and cadence sequences. Circle the notes in the scale which will be played on black keys. Practice the scale in the following rhythmic and harmonized presentation:

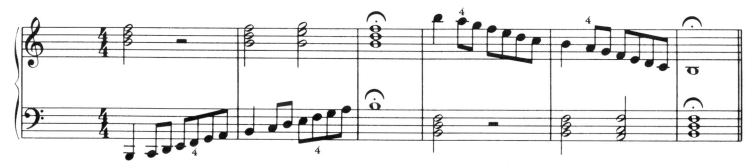

Practice the I, IV and V chords of the key of **B Major** in <u>three</u> positions, each, and the Plagal and Authentic cadences in root position. Can you tell which position of the IV chord is used in the Plagal cadence? Which position of the V chord is used in the Authentic cadence?

The following piece, **ON A QUIET LAKE**, is written in the key of **B Major**. Before you play it, write the key signature at the beginning of each staff.

ON A QUIET LAKE

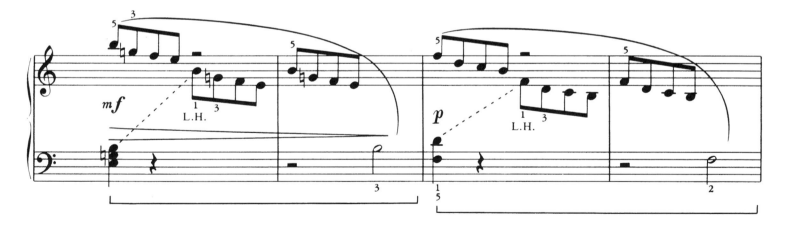

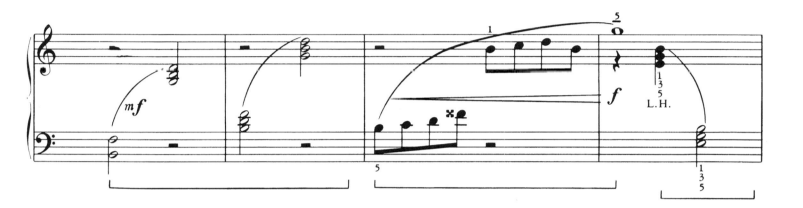

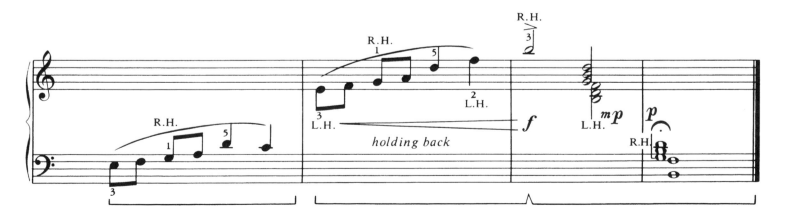

KEY OF F MAJOR

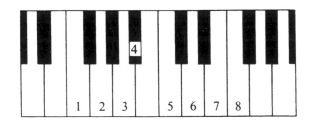

Write the names of the keys in the boxes

Here are the notes of the scale of F Major; the I, IV, V chords in root position, and two easy cadences. Write the key signature at the beginning of each staff of the scale and the chord and cadence sequences. Circle the notes in the scale which will be played on black keys. Practice the scale in the following rhythmic and harmonized presentation:

Practice the I, IV and V chords of the key of F Major in <u>three</u> positions, each, and the Plagal and Authentic cadences in root position. Can you tell which position of the IV chord is used in the Plagal cadence? Which position of the V chord is used in the Authentic cadence?

The following piece, DRUMS AND TRUMPETS, is written in the key of F Major. Before you play it, write the key signature at the beginning of each staff.

DRUMS AND TRUMPETS

With crispness and precision (♩=88-96)

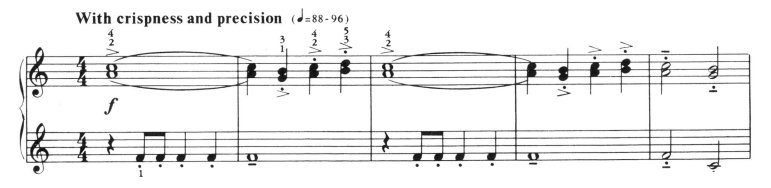

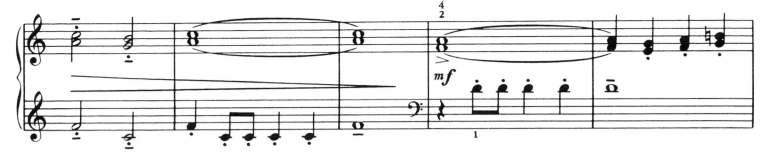

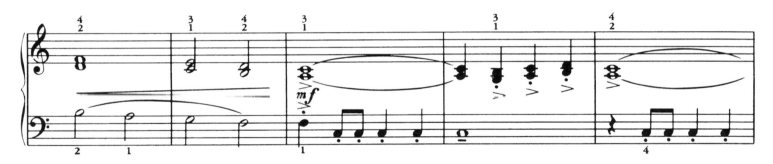

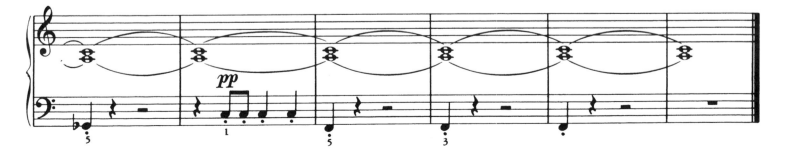

NOTES

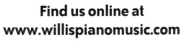